BLUES HARP & MARINE BAND
CONTENTS

Art Direction/Design
MICHAEL CONNELLY

Illustrations:
ED CACCAVALE
RUDI BATTENFELDT

Foreword

Before I started to write this book, I researched everything I could find that had been written about the *Blues Harp* and *Marine Band* harmonicas. There were many different books, and they came in all shapes, colors, and sizes. Some which were written a long time ago were simply out of date and old-fashioned. Others, surprisingly, were downright incorrect. Then there were books that were so complicated it would take a college degree in music to understand them, much less learn from them!

In all fairness, however, some books were well written, and made an honest and sincere effort to teach. In my opinion, however, these did not go far enough, so that a good deal of useful and even necessary information was left out. For instance, none of the books I checked out answered the questions I am most often asked by harmonica players. Not one has a "How-to" chapter that *really* explained repair and maintenance of the harmonica. Each of the books used its own symbols for BLOW and DRAW. This became very confusing. Some books used circles around the numbers. Some used the letters B and D, and still others used the arrow system, and even then they didn't agree. One book used an UP ↑ arrow for BLOW, and another used a DOWN ↓ arrow for the *same thing.* The method, incidentally, which is now universally accepted is an UP ↑ arrow for BLOW and a DOWN ↓ arrow for DRAW.

It soon became apparent that a need existed for a book that would answer *all* of your questions-that would "tell it like it is," and that would teach you how to fix your harmonica when it needed fixing (assuming, of course, that it's not a basket case).

Most important of all, the book should *teach you to play,* or if you already know how, should make a much better player out of you. Hopefully, this book will fill that need.

Many thanks to the Hohner Harmonica Company for their co-operation in the preparation of this book.

ALAN "BLACKIE" SCHACKNER is a composer, arranger and conductor as well as a virtuoso on the harmonica. After graduating from the New York College of Music, he attended New York University where he studied the Schillinger System of Composition under Rudolf Schramm. Mr. Schackner composed and performed the special music for William Saroyan's THE TIME OF YOUR LIFE, in which he appeared in the acting role of the newsboy. He has appeared in films, concerts, night clubs, and television with regularity, and holds the all-time record for personal appearances at the famed Concord Hotel in New York.

General Information

The music in this book is arranged specifically for the 10 hole diatonic *Marine Band* or *Blues Harp* type of harmonica in which sharps and flats *do not* naturally occur. However, the chapter on *Blues Harp* will describe how to produce your own half-steps by "bending" various notes.

It is not necessary to read music to play the melodies in this book. In addition to the musical notation, a simplified number system is provided. The number indicates the *exact* note to be played. If the arrow points up ↑ it means BLOW that note; should the arrow point down ↓ it means DRAW, or inhale. In many cases, lyrics are provided to help with the phrasing, and interpretation.

Since the 1-to-10 number system is universal for all *Marine Band* type instruments, harmonicas in *any key* can be used. It is suggested, however, that the key of **C** mouth organ be favored, since the accompaniment for guitar or piano will then be correct. If a harmonica in another key is used, the guitar or piano will have to transpose accordingly. Later on we'll explain about playing in different keys.

Whenever several numbers appear together in the music, it indicates that all of the notes are to be played simultaneously to produce a chord. The top note, which is the highest number, will always be the melody note, and should predominate.

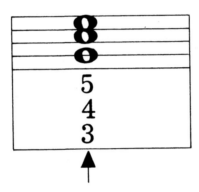

Glissando effects are very easily obtained on the harmonica, and are especially useful for flourishes and endings. They also sound professional! A glissando, or gliss, as musicians call it, is produced by starting on a low note, and rapidly sliding up to a high note. It is indicated by a wavy line: ⌣⌣⌣ . If it starts at the top of the arrow, it means start the slide upwards from the note you have just played: ↟⌣⌣ . If it starts at the bottom of the arrow, it means to start your gliss from the bottom note of the harmonica: ↡⌣⌣ . If the gliss ends on a BLOW note, it will usually be a BLOW glissando. If ending on a DRAW note, make it a DRAW glissando. These effects can also start high, and end low: ⌢⌢⌢ . The same rules apply. Experiment!

The chapter on Special Effects will explain many many more useful devices that will help your playing.

I would strongly suggest that you read the chapter on Questions and Answers before starting the actual playing.

Questions Most Often Asked About the Harmonica

Q. What exactly is the *Blues Harp?*

A. The *Blues Harp* can be *any* 10 hole, single reed, diatonic scale harmonica of the *Marine Band* category. Actually there is a harmonica specifically named the *Blues Harp*. In reality, it's a glorified *Marine Band*. It does, however, have slightly thinner reeds which are also offset somewhat more than usual, so that the player doesn't have to blow as hard. Theoretically, these reeds should bend for half-steps with less effort.

Q. So why then is the *Blues Harp* considered *different* from the *Marine Band* type harmonicas?

A. It *isn't* different, but the *manner* in which it is played is. It involves an approach which is quite unlike that of traditional harmonica playing. (This will be explained later on in the book.)

Q. Does "breaking in" a harmonica mean it has to be babied, and treated very delicately at first?

A. No, it really does not. Some books have been written which insist that the harmonica be coddled when you first play it, and even for a while afterwards. There is no scientific basis for this. Of course, I don't expect you to abuse the instrument, but if you play it as you normally would, it should give good service right from the start.

The reasons for this are easily explained. For instance, the reeds are set at the factory to vibrate at pre-determined rates. Babying doesn't change that. What does happen, however, is that moisture from your breath condenses on the wooden comb as you play. This causes it to swell slightly. Saliva, too, contributes by seeping into tiny spaces and crevices, creating a gasket-like effect which virtually eliminates any air leaks. The net result is that the instrument then "feels" better: It is more responsive, blows much easier, and the notes "bend" with less effort. This is what *really* happens when a harmonica is said to be "broken in."

Q. Is it O.K. to boil my harmonica to clean it?

A. No! Not ever! Nothing is gained by boiling. This is purely a myth that got started years ago, and has been handed down from player to player. All it does is create problems. The wooden comb swells much more than is good for the instrument. Usually, the paint peels as well, which generally results in *clogging* the reeds, which is the problem you were trying to cure in the first place. Then, too, the reeds are not too happy about the alternate heating, and cooling. So what does it accomplish? Absolutely nothing good! When the harmonica dries out, as it eventually must, it generally warps, and sometimes it even splits, ruining the instrument.

As a matter of fact, the Hohner Company (largest manufacturer of harmonicas in the world) strongly discourages the practice of boiling or soaking, and they should know. After all, the more harmonicas you boil, the more you'll buy, so when they say "Don't boil!" you can be sure it's honest advice.

Q. If I can't boil the harmonica, how DO I keep it clean?

A. By using simple common sense. Never play while chewing or eating. Try not to blow saliva into the reeds. Always tap the harmonica firmly against the palm of your hand after playing, being sure to keep the holes facing downward. This will generally clear the instrument of excess saliva, or foreign particles. Be sure to wipe the harmonica clean after using it, keeping the holes facing down, so that no lint gets into the reeds. If the harmonica is not being played, keep it in its box, case, or even wrapped in plastic.

Q. What do I do if the harmonica gets "stuck" and tapping doesn't help?

A. Good question. This happens fairly often. Generally it's caused by a speck of dust, or foreign matter jamming the reed. In most cases, it can be cleared with no harm to the harmonica, as described in the chapter on repairs.

Q. Do I have to know how to read music in order to learn to play?

A. I suppose I've been asked this question more often than any other, and the answer is an unqualified No! As a matter of fact, many of the professionals I know couldn't read a note when they started. Then again, this book uses the universally accepted arrow and number method, which is a simple, yet direct way of teaching the harmonica. If you can read music, however, it's a big help! The more you know, the better. This book will explain the fundamentals of reading music, but let's face it, learning to read is best accomplished with the aid of a qualified teacher.

Q. Why, then, do you use musical notation in addition to the numbers and arrows.

A. The answer to this is a simple one. Suppose you're not sure how long to hold a given note? Suppose you're not even sure it's the right one? You can then ask anyone who reads music on any instrument, and he, or she, can clear it up for you as easily as you read this paragraph. In addition, if someone wants to play along with you, and they do read music, it's all there.

Q. How long should it take me to *really* learn to play?

A. Well, now you've stumped the answer man. Of course, I could say that you'll play like an angel in "three easy lessons" but that would be stretching the truth a bit. You *should* be able to recognize simple tunes very quickly, but if you want to develop real expertise, much will depend on how often you practice, how musical a person you are, and how fast you learn. A Heifetz you won't become overnight, that's for sure! But if you stick with it, you *will* learn. The more you practice, the faster the progress.

Q. Do I need a lot of wind?

A. No, you don't. The mouth organ (or harmonica, if you prefer) is the only instrument which is played by both *blowing* and *drawing,* so that you're automatically breathing as you play. There are occasions where you may encounter a whole series of DRAW notes, in which case you have to learn to let some of that air escape without interfering with your playing. Sometimes the opposite will occur with a continuation of all BLOW tones. This is a problem that continually faces brass and woodwind players. Luckily this does not happen very often on the harmonica.

Q. Must I have a good "ear"?

A. By a good "ear" I assume you mean the ability to tell one note from another - or to put it another way, being able to sing, hum, or whistle a tune. Actually, it is not necessary at all! As a matter of fact, I recently read an article about a deaf mute who had learned to play simple tunes on the harmonica. He had accomplished this entirely by rote!

Most mouth organ players I know, however, *do* have excellent "ears". My own feeling is that this ability developed as they learned to play, and then became much more acute the more they practiced.

Q. Can the harmonica be tuned?

A. Theoretically, Yes. From a practical standpoint, No. Let me try to explain. We know the harmonicas have to be tuned at the factory, so that's the "Yes" part of the answer. It *can* be done, but, unfortunately, not in the same way one tunes a clarinet or trumpet.

The tuning of the harmonica reeds is a very elaborate and laborious process which requires a great deal of expertise. Special tools are required, and a set of jewelers files are a must. Then too, magnification of some sort is usually necessary in order to see what you're doing. So, for all practical purposes, the answer has to be No! Not really!

Sometimes, however, when a note drops slightly in pitch, a "touch up" *is* possible. This is explained fully in the chapter on repairs. It also describes exactly how reeds *are* tuned, should you want to try.

If you must experiment, it would be wise to use an old harmonica which has seen happier days, since at best, for the novice, tuning reeds is a calculated risk.

Q. Which is better, the *Chromatic Harmonica,* or the *Blues Harp?*

A. Well! Now you're asking abut apples and oranges. You really can't compare the two. They're distinctly different.

Even the sounds produced are not quite the same. For instance the *Harp* has a somewhat thinner tone than that of the chromatic, the sound of which is generally rounder and more full "Mellow" might best describe it. Then, too, notes on the *Blues Harp* are easier to bend and have a "funky" quality. The overall result is a sound that is quite different from that of the chromatic harmonica. (I find it no problem to tell them apart.)

The *Harp* is purely diatonic in nature, the scale of which consists of but seven notes, while its chromatic brother boasts twelve. Even if we consider adding the extra notes on the *Harp* which are obtained by bending, the instrument must still be limited to certain types of music. This should not be considered a handicap, however, since the diatonic harmonica lends itself admirably to the simple, honest, unpretentious kind of music which is so popular today. It also requires much less expertise, and is much easier to master and to play. The chromatic harmonica, on the other hand, is a complete musical instrument, capable of tone colors and effects not easily duplicated on any other single instrument, regardless of size. With it, a skilled player can play almost anything, and in any key. If he (or she) has really done his homework, he can read music at sight, as easily as you read this. The possibilities are only limited by the player himself. The instrument can just about do it all! So you see, it's not reasonable to compare the two. I consider them distinctly different instruments. A chapter in this book is devoted entirely to the chromatic harmonica. It explains in much more detail.

Q. What are harmonica reeds made of?

A. A special alloy of brass designed specifically for this purpose.

Q. Why don't they make the reeds of steel, or some of the new very strong plastics? Wouldn't they last longer?

A. In the case of plastics, the answer is an unqualified No. Many plastic reeds have been tried. None have held up nearly so well as what we now utilize. They fail in tone quality, as well as resiliency. As for steel, it's strong all right. Too strong! Those that have been tried have been much too hard to blow, and besides, *they rust!* So why not *stainless* steel? Not nearly flexible enough. Then, too, there are technical limitations pertaining to the size of the reeds, metalurgical considerations and so forth. So for the immediate future, brass seems to be our best bet.

When one considers the speed at which reeds vibrate, it's remarkable that they hold up as well as they do. For example, **A** above middle **C** vibrates at 440 CPS (cycles per second). As we ascend the scale, the speed of the vibrations increase in a direct mathematical ratio, so that the octave above **A** when sounded, oscillates at 880 times a second. If we go still further up the scale, say to the high **C** on the *Marine Band* harmonica, and activate that reed, it will be found to vibrate at the incredible rate of *2093 times per second!* Really amazing!

Q. Are harmonicas guaranteed?

A. Yes, but not against *usage.* They are warranteed to be free from manufacturing defects or other noticeable imperfections at the time of purchase. This also applies to the tuning of the instrument. If it's out of tune when you get it, the factory should repair or replace the harmonica at no cost to the purchaser.

Q. How long should a harmonica last?

A. I couldn't possibly answer that. There are so many variables. Some harmonicas last for years. Others sometimes fail prematurely. If you play very hard, or very loud, and do a lot of bending of notes, don't expect your *Harp* to last as long as the mouth organ of a player who plays softly, and with sensitivity.

Q. Do the harmonica companies repair *used* harmonicas?

A. Hohner Company does this, but I don't know about other manufacturers. The usual procedure is to send the harmonica to the factory, enclosing a note to explain the problem. They will then advise what charges are involved, and await your decision as to whether you want it returned "as is" or repaired. Sometimes only a slight adjustment is necessary. In that case, the harp will be returned free of charge. Most of the time the difficulties are of a minor nature, and, if the user knows what to look for, easily corrected.

Q. Do manufacturers sell individual spare parts?

A. No, they do not.

Q. Must I learn to play straight harmonica before I can play *Blues Harp?*

A. Absolutely!!! You can't run before you can walk, and playing blues is merely a variation of the normal function of the harmonica. The playing *technique* is basically the same.

Q. In what keys are the *Marine Band* harmonicas made?

A. They are now available in *all* the keys. (**A, Bb, C, Db, D, Eb, E, F, F#, G,** and **Ab**)

Q. Why so many keys? Trumpets and clarinets don't come in twelve keys.

A. True. But because of the diatonic nature of the *Harp* (a 7-tone scale without chromatic intervals,) you can only play straight *Harp* in the key to which your harmonica is tuned. Therefore, if you want to play in the key of **Db,** you would normally require a **Db** *Harp.* The trumpet and clarinet are *chromatic* in nature (they provide all of the half-steps necessary), so you can play in *any* key on the instrument. This is also true for the *chromatic* harmonica. It, too, can play in any key.

Q. Are there any other harmonicas I should know about in the *Marine Band* category?

A. Yes. There are two brand new harmonicas, respectively called *Golden Melody* and *Special 20*. Both of these harps have a plastic body. This feature completely eliminates the problem of wood swelling. In addition, compression on both harps is excellent, which makes for easy bending. They are available in all the keys, and are priced slightly higher than the *Marine Band*. Players who play with a very wet mouth should certainly find these harps very helpful. Preliminary response both by amateurs and professionals, has been very enthusiastic.

Q. What about the Echo harmonicas? Since they have double holes and two reeds tuned to the same note, wouldn't they be better?

A. Again, we're talking about apples and oranges. These harmonicas are fine, and sound something like a French Accordion. They're also somewhat louder. They are not, however, suitable for playing blues, or for bending notes.

Q. Can you quote prices for some of the harmonicas you are writing about?

A. Not really! Because of recent world wide economic uncertainties, chances are, by the time you read this, any prices I might give would be out of date. Shop around! Many stores give discounts.

Q. Can I test a harmonica in the store *before* I buy it?

A. An excellent question! Especially since this has caused problems both for the storekeeper and the player. The answer is Yes, but *not by playing the harmonica!* Once you take a harmonica into your mouth to play it, you've bought it! Most stores, however have a special harmonica tester that works by bellows action. It can check out a harmonica quite efficiently. If by chance you should get a faulty harmonica, don't get mad at the guy who sold it to you. It's not his fault, and he *can't* change it for you. All he can do is send it back to the factory, and you'd be better off doing that yourself. It's a lot faster. Just describe the problem. The factory wants you to be happy, and they'll bend over backward to keep you that way. Don't try sending them a beat up old harp, and claim you just bought it. They're experts! Incidentally, the chances of getting a *bad* harmonica are very slight, especially if you use the bellows tester.

Q. Is there any difference between the terms *Harp, Mouth Organ,* and *Harmonica?*

A. No. They all mean exactly the same thing.

Learning to Play the Harmonica

Introduction

A few pertinent comments before we actually start to learn: Your harmonica, although tiny, is very cleverly constructed. The notes are already in tune, and arranged in such a way that just blowing into the *Harp* in any position results in a perfectly fine chord. It is literally impossible to create a discord. If you've ever tried to play a trumpet, clarinet, or violin you can appreciate what this means. No long period of time is required to learn to "make" the notes. They are already on the mouth organ, just waiting to be sounded. Play them in proper sequence, and you have music!

Your harmonica has one other important advantage: It is really portable. You can enjoy it wherever you go, and when you consider the fun you'll get from it, you can appreciate that any time you may spend learning to play will more than pay off in pleasure derived.

Holding The Harmonica

The first thing to learn about the harmonica is the correct way to hold it. The low notes should *always* be on your left as you play. (You can check this simply by blowing into the harmonica.) The basic position will never vary, although how the harmonica is held in your hands depends on what is most comfortable and natural for you. No two players hold their *Harps* exactly alike. Generally though, the harmonica is held in the left hand, while the right hand takes care of the vibrato, tremolo, or even cupping effects. The accompanying sketches suggest several possiblilities. Try them! Then pick the one that suits you best.

Basic Hand Positions:

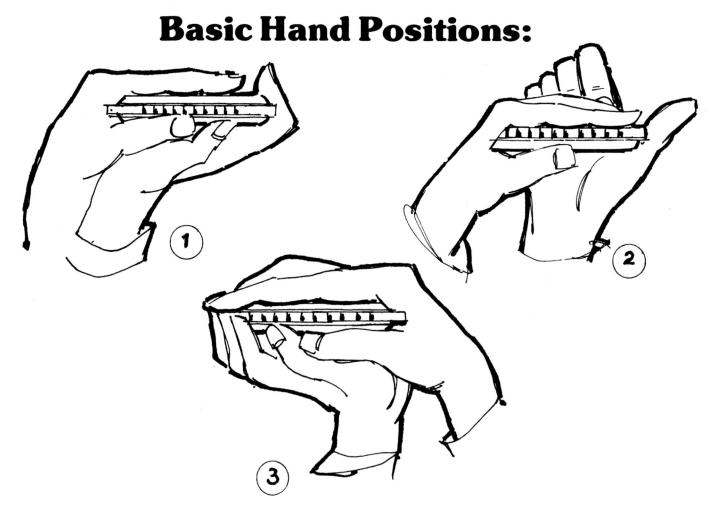

Holding your *Harp,* easily and naturally, blow and draw on it lightly. You will hear several pleasant sounding chords. You might keep this up for a few moments just to get the "feel" of the harmonica. However, sounding a full chord (several notes at the same time) is *not* your goal at this point. Instead, the most important first step is learning to play but one note at a time. This sometimes gives beginners a bit of trouble, but once this step is mastered, everything else falls into place much more easily.

Sounding A Note

There are two ways that you can play a single note. The easiest is the pursed lips method in which the lips just cover a single note. This type of playing is generally referred to as "lipping". If you think of drinking a soda through a straw, your lips will automatically be in the proper position. Lipping is very useful in playing Blues Harp and in bending notes.

"Lipping"

Lips are pursed only over note to be sounded.
Tongue does not touch harmonica.

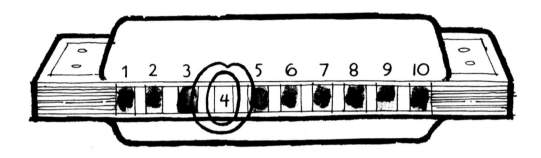

Although the *Marine Band* type harmonica has *ten* holes, for the moment, we will not be concerned with any notes below hole #4. Also, in order to avoid any confusion in notation, (names of the notes, **C, D, E,** etc.) it is suggested that you use a key of **C** Harp, although the following procedures will work in *any* key!

Tongue Blocking

Inner circle indicates tongue which blocks holes 1, 2 and 3.
Outer line indicates mouth.

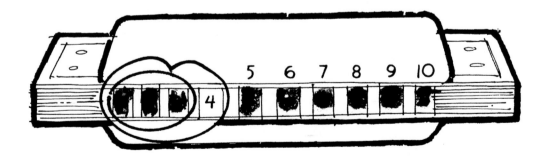

Note that hole #4 remains open but 1, 2 and 3 are blocked.

The second method, which is used much more often, especially by professionals, is called tongue blocking, because the mouth covers four holes, the tongue blocks three, and the remaining hole is the one that is sounded. Tongue blocking is a little more difficult to learn, but will also prove useful, especially if you eventually want to progress to the *chromatic harmonica.*

PLAYING THE SCALE: Lipping Method

Using the lipping method, try blowing into hole #4. There should be nothing forced or strained about this. Just blow lightly and naturally, almost like breathing. You should then hear a *single* note. If you are correct, that will be the first note of the scale, or **DO.** To make certain that you've done this properly, check yourself by covering holes 1, 2, and 3 with the index finger of your left hand, and holes 5 through 10 with the index finger of your right. Obviously this leaves only hole #4 open. Blow into it lightly, and you'll hear the note **C** or **DO.** You can use this device to check yourself as you proceed, being sure to leave open only that particular note you're trying to sound. It is *very important* that you learn to play a single note at a time before continuing.

Since we have already played the **C** or BLOW 4, the next note must be **D (RE)** or DRAW 4. Move the harmonica slightly to the left, and BLOW 5 which results in **E (MI).** DRAWING on the 5th hole then gives the **F** or **FA.** The rest of the scale is merely a continutation. BLOW 6 is **G** or **SOL,** and DRAW 6 makes the **A** or **LA.** On hole 7, however, there is one important *difference.* Here you DRAW first to obtain the **B** or **TI,** and then BLOW to complete the scale with the **C** or **DO.**

"Lipping"

Lips are pursed only over note to be sounded.

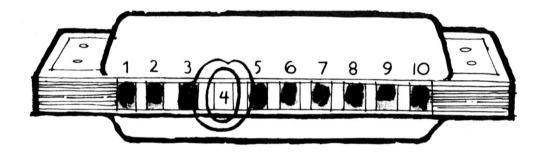

Tongue does not touch the harmonica.

PLAYING THE SCALE: Tongue Blocking Method

If you prefer more practice using the lipping method before you learn the two tongue blocking methods, skip the next paragraphs until you've mastered the first piece of music, TAPS.

If not, start again with hole #4. This time your mouth covers four holes, with your tongue blocking three holes, so that only hole #4 is left open to play. Again, just blow naturally, and do it as many times as necessary to make the note play easily. This may be a little frustrating at first, but don't become discouraged. Remember that thousands of people have mastered the harmonica, so why shouldn't you?

Now go back to playing the scale, only this time using tongue blocking. Practice this until you can play it with assurance and authority. Learn to play it backwards as well, until it all comes naturally, and it will!

FOR THE SAKE OF CLARITY AND BREVITY, ALL BLOW NOTES WILL BE INDICATED BY AN ARROW POINTING UP ↑ AND DRAW NOTES BY AN ARROW POINTING DOWN ↓ (This is the universally accepted method of number notation developed by the M. HOHNER COMPANY.

Tongue Blocking

Inner circle indicates tongue which blocks holes 1, 2 and 3.
Outer line indicates mouth.

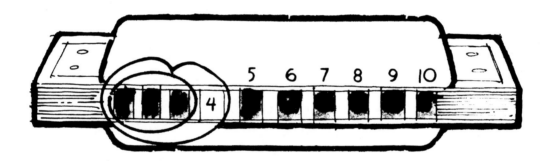

Note that hole #4 remains open but 1, 2 and 3 are blocked.

A complete diagram of the scale, both ascending and descending appears below. All numbers, names, and musical notation are included.

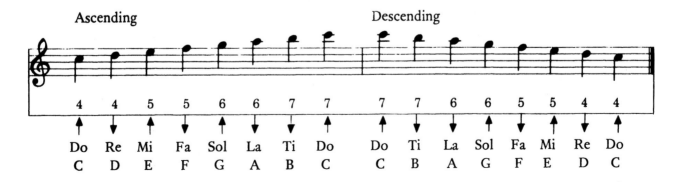

	Ascending								Descending							
	4	4	5	5	6	6	7	7	7	7	6	6	5	5	4	4
	↑	↓	↑	↓	↑	↓	↓	↑	↑	↓	↓	↑	↓	↑	↓	↑
	Do	Re	Mi	Fa	Sol	La	Ti	Do	Do	Ti	La	Sol	Fa	Mi	Re	Do
	C	D	E	F	G	A	B	C	C	B	A	G	F	E	D	C

Playing All the Notes

Thus far, you have utilized only eight notes of the twenty that are available on your harmonica. (Each hole contains two reeds, and you've used 4, 5, 6, and 7.) It is only natural then, that you've become curious about the function of the rest of your harmonica. The answers are simple. Although holes 1, 2, and 3 do not form a complete scale, they do form two perfectly fine chords (**C** and **G**). So those notes are often, *but not always,* used for accompaniments and "umpah" effects to simple melodies. This type of playing is called "tonguing" and can only be performed when tongue blocking. (The tongue is lifted on and off the harmonica in tempo to the type of song being played. Years ago, this style of playing was very popular. Today it is still used but mostly in country music.) Holes 1, 2, and 3 are also very useful in playing *Blues Harp*. More about this in the chapter on playing *Blues*.

Since you've already explored holes 4 through 7 (the primary scale) you need to discover the function of holes 8, 9, and 10. They are simply a continuation of the scale. If you DRAW 8 you'll sound the **D.** BLOW 8 gives the **E.** DRAW 9 results in an **F,** and BLOW 9, **G.** By DRAWING hole 10 the **A** will be heard, and BLOWING 10 *almost* completes the scale by sounding the **C.** Note, however, that there is no **B** in the upper register. This is due to the construction of the harmonica. See sketch No. 6 which gives the complete layout of your *Harp*.

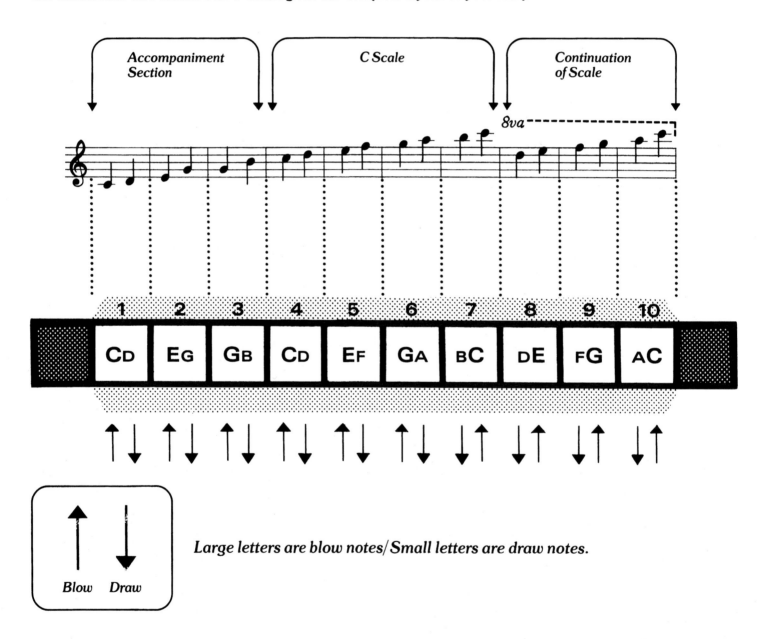

Large letters are blow notes/Small letters are draw notes.

By this time you should be reasonably familiar with the scale, so why not proceed to the next step: Actually play a melody! For a first attempt, try a very simple tune that everybody knows, namely, "Taps". If you look at the illustration for "Taps", you'll notice that it is made up of BLOW notes only. In this case, no guitar accompaniment is included, since "Taps" is always played unaccompanied. (All other melodies *will* include chord symbols, just in case you have a friend who plays guitar or piano, and wants to help out.) However, for your convenience, the numbers, and actual notes are included.

Taps

This simple melody should be played lightly, and with feeling. The symbol ⌒ that occasionally appears, merely means that you are to hold that note a little longer than the note value would indicate. The word RITARD. directs you to hold back, or play a little more slowly at that point.

Taps (High Register)

"Taps" can also be played an octave lower by borrowing a note from the accompaniment section, and starting on hole #3.

Remember to try to produce a *single* tone at all times. Interestingly enough, the famous bugle call "Taps" will sound good even if you *don't* quite succeed in sounding that elusive single note. So if you're having problems, this should encourage you. But don't let it go to your head. Practice this until you *can* do it in single notes!

Taps (Low Register)

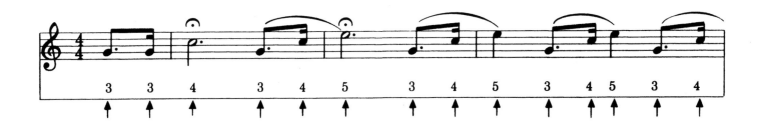

How Dry I Am

Another simple tune that you should try after you've mastered the playing of "Taps" is the famous barroom ditty "How Dry I Am," Notice that this time, several DRAW notes are included. This should be no problem at all. Mouth positions remain the same as when BLOWING. Just be certain that you're playing the notes that are indicated. Incidentally, this tune is just perfect for using the "wah wah" effect. (Later on in this book, all of these special effects like bending, wah wah, glissandos, and many more, will be explained in detail.) You'll find using some of these tricks a lot of fun, and they'll help you to sound professional as well.

In the pages that follow, you'll find several songs written out for you. In these, we have used the number and arrrow method of notation. All of these tunes include lyrics, guitar or piano accompaniment, and even the actual musical notation. Should you be in doubt about the rhythm, or the feeling of any of these songs, the lyrics will generally give you all the help you'll need. If however, you're still in doubt, you can ask anyone who reads music on *any* instrument and it's all there.

Some of these songs may require a bit more practice than others, but the results will be well worth it. For instance, if you play "Dixie" to a Southern audience, I guarantee you'll automatically get a standing ovation! Then, if you'd like to give equal time to the opposition, play "Yankee Doodle"! And just in case that doesn't work, we've even included an arrangement of the "Battle Hymn of the Republic" (a crowd pleaser as good as any I've ever heard).

I've also arranged two good old standards which will introduce you to the technique of "tonguing", a very useful form of self accompaniment. The songs are: "When the Saints Go Marching In", and "Polly Wolly Doodle". Incidentally, if you've practiced your tongue blocking, you should automatically be able to tongue! Just lift your tongue to include the accompaniment notes, then put it back on the harmonica again to sound just the single note. That's really all there is to it! Just remember to do this in a rhythmic pattern to suit the tune that you happen to be playing. I've indicated several possibilities in the tunes I've arranged. Experiment! Try some rhythms of your own. Eventually you'll develop a useful technique.

If you're wondering why this type of playing is not used more often, its because the chords available on the harmonica (tonic and dominant) do not always fit the melody being played. This is especially true for the more sophisticated kinds of songs in which the harmonies are quite involved. However, there are many times when these chords *will* fit, especially in country and folk music, and then this effect comes in very handy. All harmonica players should include it in their bag of tricks.

Yankee Doodle

Note: (Actual notation is an octave higher)

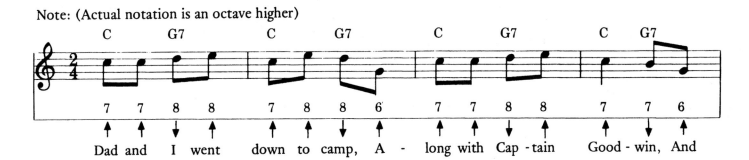

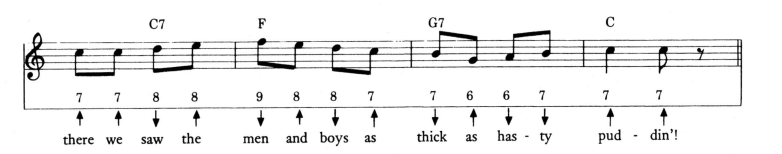

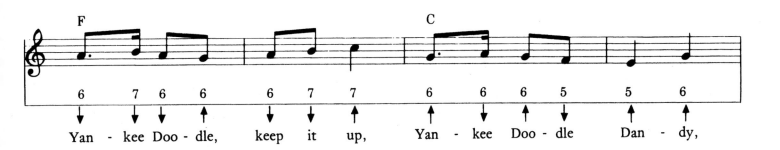

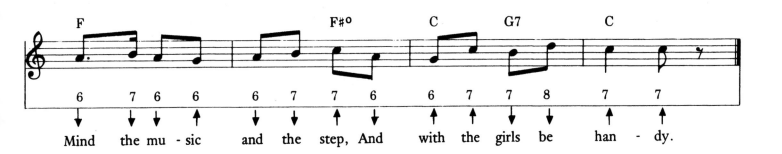

Battle Hymn of The Republic

Note: (Actual notation is an octave higher)

March tempo

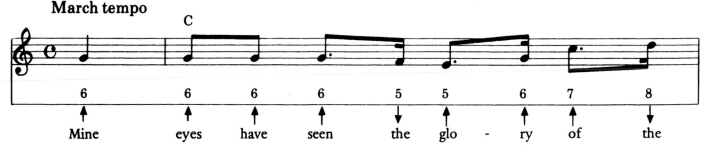

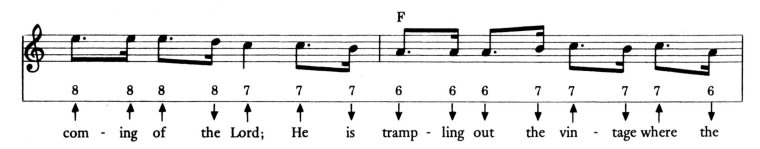

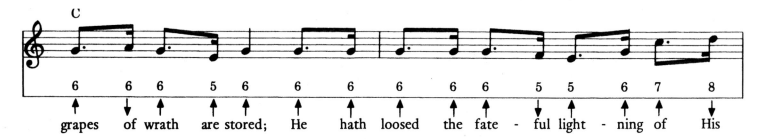

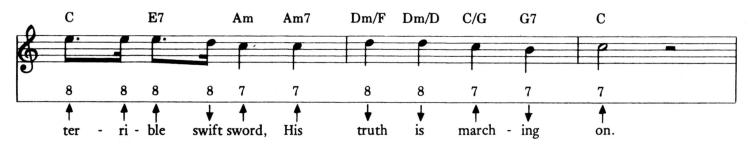

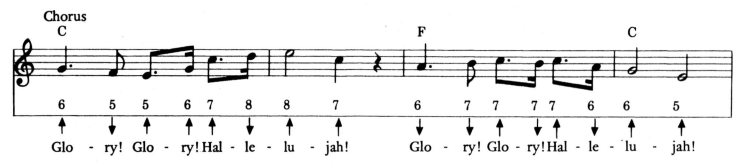

Dixie

Note: (Actual notation is an octave higher)

When The Saints Go Marching In

This next arrangement, "When the Saints Go Marching In", is an exercise in "tonguing". Remember to use the tongue blocking method. Play the single note first, then simply lift your tongue to include the accompaniment chord. Naturally, when you put your tongue back on the harmonica, the chord will cut off, but the single note should sustain. I've indicated a simple but effective rhythmic accompaniment. Practice this. It's really a very nice effect.

"Polly Wolly Doodle" is another example of a tune that is perfectly harmonized for self accompaniment (tonguing). Incidentally, this does not mean that another instrument can't accompany you as well. As a matter of fact, "Polly" will sound even better if a guitar, piano, organ, (or whatever) joins you. But if you don't happen to have one of these instrumentalists around, the technique of tonguing makes you completely self sufficient.

In the 13th and 14th measures of this song (the part that says; "Goin' to Louisana for to see my Susyanna", you will notice that instead of single notes, two notes at a time are indicated. These are called "double stops". The top note is always the melody, and the second note is harmony. These double stops can be played either by lipping, or tongue blocking. You'll probably find that for the beginner, lipping is easier. Just play *two* notes instead of one. If you want to do this by tongue blocking, you have to move your tongue slightly to the left, again, in order to let *two* notes sound instead of one. Ideally, you should learn to play double stops both ways.

Polly Wolly Doodle

Oh, I went down south for to see my Sal, Sing ___ Pol - ly Wol - ly Doo - dle all the day. My ___ Sal - ly am a ___ spunk - y gal, Sing Pol - ly Wol - ly Doo - dle all the day. Fare thee well, Fare thee well. Fare thee well my Fair - y Fay, For I'm goin' to Lou - si - an - a for to see my Sus - y - an - na, Sing Pol - ly Wol - ly Doo - dle all the day. ___

And now that you're well on your way to playing straight harmonica, let's go on to the *Blues Harp!*

The Blues Harp

First, let's clear up some of the confusion about the names and terms that are used. When we refer to the *Blues Harp* we're not just talking about the harmonica of that name, but, a style of playing that pertains to *all Marine Band* type harmonicas that are made with *single* reeds, and can be played in "Cross Harp" positions.

Now to explain what is meant by Cross Harp, which includes positions 2 through 6: If you refer to the chapter on Straight Harp, you'll notice that the harmonica plays in the exact key to which it is tuned. A **C** harmonica plays in the key of **C**. Straight harp is also referred to as 1st position. Cross Harp simply means playing your harmonica in a different key then the one to which it is tuned. For instance, if you play your key of **C** harp in the key of **G**, you'll be playing Cross Harp in the *2nd* position. This, incidentally, is the one most often used to play The Blues.

Originally, "The Blues" meant a slow, *minor* key type of music that often reflected a feeling of sadness. Today, especially when played on the harmonica, Blues can be exciting, creative, and even make you feel *good!* Also, in contrast to the old minor key flavor, the most often used chord combinations now are in *Major* keys.

The basic Blues progression is made up of just three chords. These chords are built on the 1st, 4th, and 5th notes of the scale (diatonic). It's not really necessary that you know any of this but the more you know...

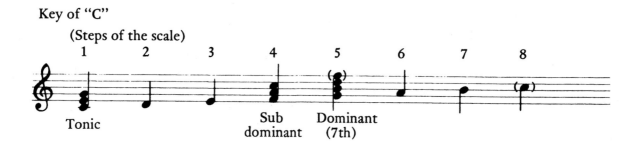

The chords in this diagram can be called the I, IV, and V7 or the Tonic, Subdominant and Dominant 7th. If you were to play in the key of **C**, the exact chord names would be **C, F** and **G7th**. All of these are just different ways of saying *exactly the same thing!* While there are variations of this pattern, these three chords form the basis from which all Blues develop.

If you happen to be playing your **C** harp in the key of **G**, which is the 2nd position, all of this would still hold true except that the tonic would then be a **G** chord, the Sub-dominant a **C** chord, and the Dominant 7th would then be called a **D7th**. No matter what key you happen to be playing in, the Tonic, Sub-dominant, and Dominant 7th are always built on the 1st, 4th, and 5th steps of the diatonic scale of that particular key.

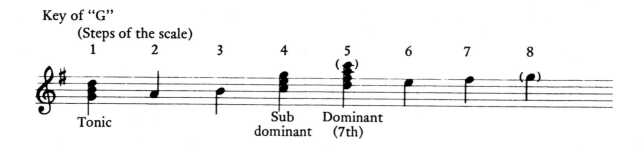

Straight Harmonica Blues

The basic Blues pattern runs twelve measures long. It is generally in 4/4 time, which means each measure gets 4 beats or foot taps, if that's easier. The following example is typical. It happens to be in 1st position (Straight Harp). We've kept it quite simple, and a lyric has been added to help you with the rhythmic pattern. This tune, which we've named "Straight Harp Blues", should acquaint you with the basic Blues "feel". (As yet, no bending! Remember? First we walk, *then* we run.)

1st Position, Key of C
on a C Harmonica

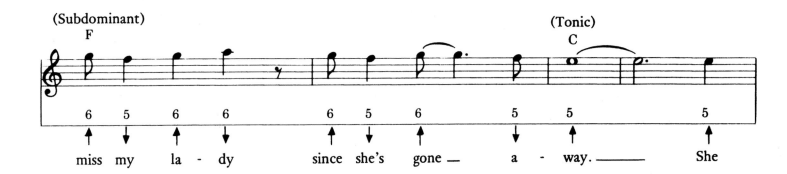

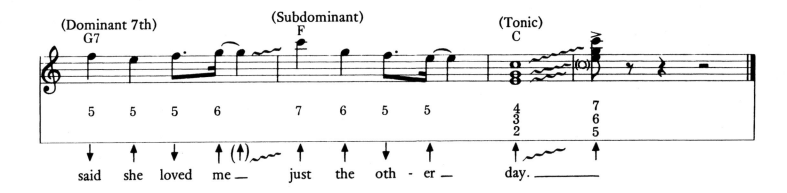

Bending Notes

The foregoing example sounds perfectly OK in the 1st position (Straight Harp), but you'll notice that we're pretty well limited to single notes above hole 4 except for the chord glissando at the end, which is nothing more than window dressing. The reason for this is that from hole 4 upwards, we have a complete scale, while in the lower register, the **F** and the **A** are *missing,* and since we needed those notes, we were forced to stay in the upper register. Later on, you'll learn how to "make" those missing notes, and more, by bending. Another reason why "Straight Harp" doesn't quite make it for Blues is that some of the notes we most want to bend happen to be BLOW notes, and they're very very difficult to bend, especially below hole 7. On the other hand, most DRAW tones are relatively easy. Then, too, in Cross Harp (2nd position) when you draw a mouthful of notes, (holes 2, 3, 4 and 5) you automatically hear the Tonic chord with an added 7th, which happens to be a very convenient, built in, Blues sound, and quite impossible in the first position. So, now that you know some of the reasons why, lets work on Cross Harp, 2nd position.

(There seems to be some confusion among players, and books as well, about which position is 1st, and which is 2nd. Some books refer to 2nd position as 1st position Cross Harp. Logically, 1st position is key of **C** on a **C** harmonica, which is, of course, Straight Harp, as we've explained. Anyway, it doesn't matter what you call it, as long as you know how to play it!)

Since we're going to start "bending" notes in the next example, I may as well explain exactly what it all means, and how it's done.

A note is bent by changing your mouth position in such a way that you *lower* the natural pitch of a note. Lower it slightly and you can produce a "wah-wah" effect. Pulsate it that way, and you have a vibrato. Lower it more, and you'll actually "make" a note that doesn't really exist on the instrument. Some notes can be bent as much as 3 half steps *lower* than normal, while others can't be bent at all, or at least not without great difficulty.

Notes can only be *lowered* from their natural pitch. They *cannot be raised. You can make a note seem* to bend up however, by starting it in the bent position, and letting it come up to its natural pitch.

So much for explanations. Now how do you do it? Easy! A good note to start on is DRAW 4. Use the "lipping" position, since it's easier then tongue blocking for most people. As you DRAW, silently form the word "wah-oo-wah". This produces the simple "wah-wah" effect, and is actually the basis for all bending. Now let's break it down!

As you say "wah", your hand should be in an *open* position. When you say "oo", you *cup* your hands, then open them again for the last "wah". This all takes place as fast as you can say wahoowah! Think of it as this way:

wah	**oo**	**wah**
open	**cupped**	**open**

When you form the oo sound, your lips should jut forward a little. At the same time, your cheeks should tighten up, so that the air chamber in your mouth is reduced, and the opening between your lips should become much smaller, (something like sucking on a straw when something suddenly clogs it). If I were to draw an exaggerated diagram of the lip opening, it might look like this:

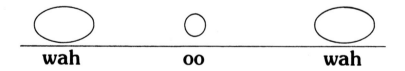

| **wah** | **oo** | **wah** |

It is *not* necessary to force the breath, or to draw very hard, since this can be accomplished softly, as well as with more volume.

That's really all there is to it, but it will require patience, so don't become discouraged. You *will* succeed!

Since you want to go further, and produce some of the missing half tones, you have to bend the note even more. This is done by tightening up even more on the "oo" part of the sound. The symbol we'll use when we want you to bend a note; is a *BENT* arrow. It will look like this:

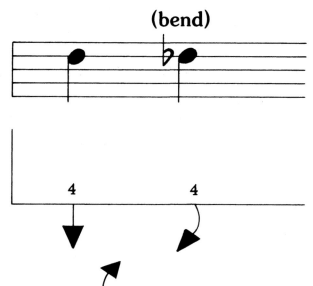

If it's a BLOW note, it will be pointing up: A DRAW note will point down. (It will also be indicated musically as well, just in case you need some musical assistance.)

Now let's try bending some other notes. You'll find that the DRAW notes from 1 to 7 bend fairly easily, but from 8 to 10, they resist bending. OK so far, but what about the BLOW notes? Pretty tough! Especially in the low register. Strangely enough, from 7 on up, the BLOW notes bend pretty easily. So, experiment! Try bending, using both the lipping and tongue blocking methods. In some cases, on some notes tongue-blocking may actually be easier!

Another good effect is to start on the lowered or bent note, then slide up to the natural pitch. This sounds like the note is being bent *upwards!* You can also learn to bend two, or even three notes at the same time. This is done in exactly the same way as ordinary bending, except that your mouth will have to cover two (or three) notes instead of one. This trick is particularly useful in playing Blues. Experiment! You'll be surprised at what you come up with. Try hitting a note normally, then bend it, and come back with a separation in between each tone, so that they sound like separate and distinctly different notes. To do this with a sharp attack, say (silently)

tah	**too**	**tah**
normal	**bent**	**normal**

Since DRAW 4 is the easiest hole to start on, be sure to master it first before tackling some of the more difficult notes. The chapter on special effects will explain some of the other interesting sounds you can produce, like shakes, trills, vibrato, and such.

Since bending notes can sometimes be very difficult and frustrating, I'm often asked if soaking the harmonica in water helps to make bending easier. The answer is a qualified yes. It does help some, because it causes the wooden comb to swell, which in turn improves the compression. But it also shortens the life of the harmonica! In addition, it voids the guarantee. Then, too, if the comb happens to be made of plastic as in the Golden Melody harp, soaking won't accomplish a thing! It's your harmonica. The choice is yours.

Cross Harp Blues

The next example, which we've named "Cross Harp Blues", has two notes at the end that call for bending. They're both easy notes, and shouldn't give you any trouble. Also in this example, we use double stops (two notes at a time) throughout a good part of the tune. These are so constructed that even if you should overlap or not play the notes exactly "on the nose", they will still sound good. Even without accompaniment, this example will sound "full". The notes that are in brackets ( ) are optional, but try to play them. They'll help you to sound professional. Your **C** harmonica will now be playing in the key of **G**.

2nd Position, Key of G
played on a Key of C Harmonica

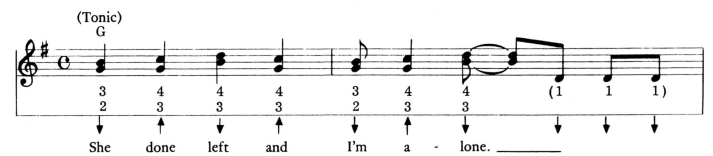

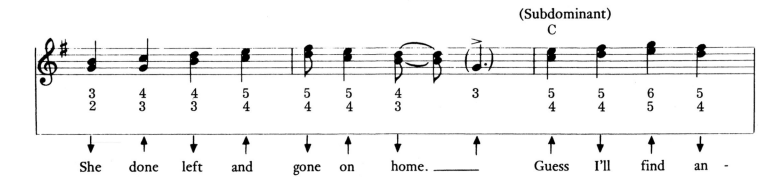

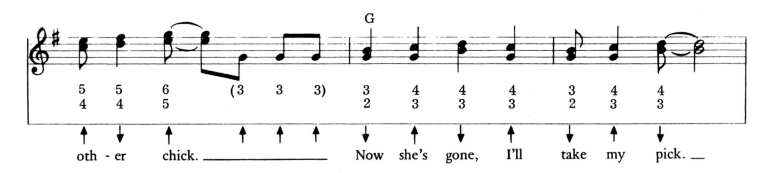

3rd Position Blues

"Cross Harp Blues" is played in the *2nd* position, the position you'll use most often. It's the easiest and most convenient. Master this position first before going to the next step, which will of course be in the *3rd* position, and is named just that: "3rd Position Blues". You'll notice that in this tune, we stay mostly around holes 4 to 6, and we only have to bend two easy notes; DRAW 4 (the easiest of all) and DRAW 6. This should cause you no problems. Your **C** harp will now be playing in the key of **D**.

Key of D played on a Key of "C" Harmonica

4th Position Blues

Most *Blues Harp* players generally quit after 3 positions, but actually there are *3 more positions* not only possible, but in many cases, quite practical as well. And just to prove the point, we've included examples of each!

This next sample (4th position) puts you in the key of **E** on a **C** Harp, yet you only have to bend one double stop, and still wind up with a perfectly fine blues "feel". The bend, which happens to be a wah-wah, occurs on holes 3 and 4 simultaneously. Both notes bend quite easily, and since they happen to be the 5th and 7th notes of the Tonic chord in **E**, they help quite a bit to give us the Blues sound. The other note that you bend in this example is DRAW 6. By this time that should be familiar to you since we used it in the last example.

Key of E on a Key of "C" Harmonica

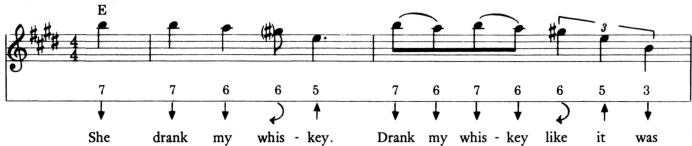

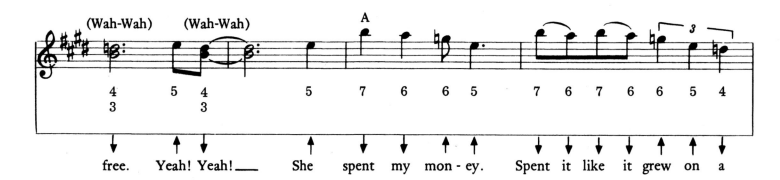

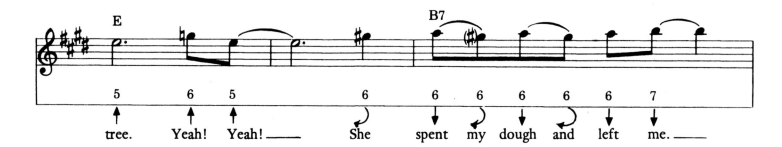

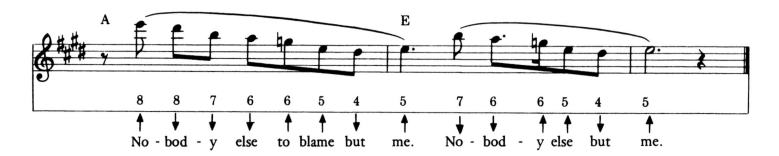

5th Position Blues

5th position puts your **C** harmonica in the key of **A**. In the example that follows, you'll be bending a BLOW note for the first time. In this particular case, it happens to be BLOW 8. If you were to attempt to bend BLOW 5, which is the same note an octave lower, you would find it almost impossible. As a matter of fact, this entire illustration would be very awkward if not impossible in the low register, so we do it up high, where everything falls into place very nicely. Notice too, that BLOW 8 is attacked in the bent position, and allowed to slide *up* to the natural pitch of the note. The syllables to use (silently, of course) are "too-wah". Try this, both tongue blocking and lipping. One will probably be easier for you.

Key of A on a "C" Harmonica

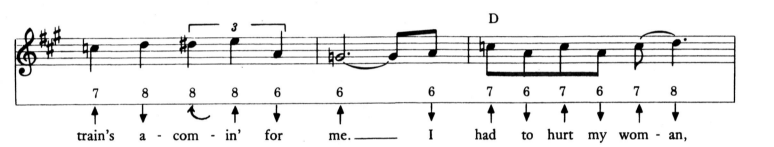

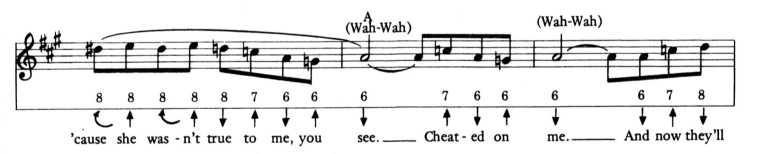

6th Position Blues

And now we come to the last position, which is #6. This puts your **C** Harp in the key of **F**. Strangely enough, many of the notes you'll need are already on the harmonica, and in this illustration, you only have to bend *one* note. Although you are already familiar with this particular bend (DRAW 6), this example may prove a little bit more difficult, because you don't have much time to pucker up. It then becomes a matter of practice. Also, on the BLOW 7, DRAW 7, BLOW 7 which happens only once in this tune, you might prefer to BLOW 7, *BEND* BLOW 7, and then play BLOW 7 naturally. The notes will be the same, but the second way will sound more "Bluesy".

Key of F on a "C" Harmonica

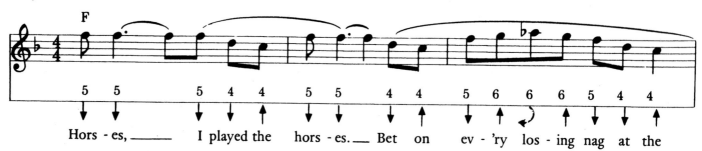

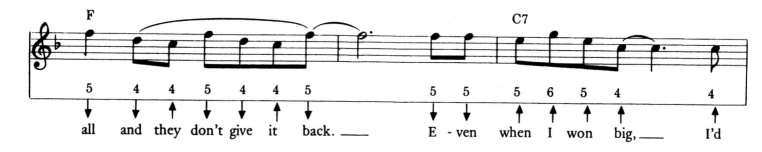

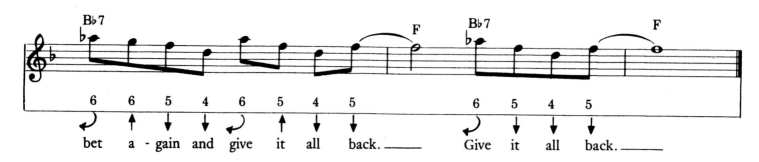

In all of the foregoing examples, we've given you complete, and self-sufficient solos to play. This is not to suggest that you'll be able to play *every* song in all six positions. On the contrary, in most situations you'll find that you have to improvise *around* the melody, even in *2nd* position. Some combinations of notes are just not practical if not altogether impossible on the harp. Then too, sometimes you'll find yourself playing accompaniment to someone else's solo performance. In that case, you don't have to play as many notes, just an occasional fill, "wah wah", or what have you. It's much easier.

Fills

The playing of "fills" means pretty much what the word itself implies: filling in the pauses and empty spots in someone else's performance. What you play is purely a matter of personal taste, and taste is acquired by listening. Sometimes a single, simple note is enough. Other times a few well chosen double stops, or a "wah wah" or two may be right. It all depends on what else is going on musically. The best way to learn, and to get all this together, is to listen, listen and then listen some more to as many *Harp* players as you can, especially those whose work you admire. You should remember however, that when playing fills, you're only the seasoning (like salt and pepper on a main dish). Help the soloist, but don't over spice the performance!

When playing accompaniment, the same general rules will apply, except that you'll often play right through the tune, using longer, sustained notes and chords where practical.

All sorts of recordings are available, and most good record shops have a rack specifically set aside just for harmonica buffs. If you like a particular record, don't be afraid to imitate somebody else's style. That's how we *all* started. Eventually, as you learn and progress, your *own* style will emerge!

The daddy of all the *Blues Harp* players is, of course, Sonny Terry. Listen to some of his work. It's really great! Charlie McCoy is another fine Harp player, who, although he specializes in country music, can wail along with the best. You should also listen to any recordings by Paul Butterfield. There are many, many others. All of the players mentioned will, and should influence your playing. You can get many new and fresh ideas from them.

One good way to learn is to play along with a recording. If you do, it's a good idea to have a variable speed control on your phono. Sometimes the speed of the platter, or phono motor, is slightly off, making the recording flat, sharp, or even in the wrong key. A speed control would help to correct this. Also, if you're trying to copy a phrase or a group of notes from a recording, and the whole thing is moving too fast for you to pick anything out, set your machine for 16-2/3 RPM. (I'm assuming that you have a four speed phono.) This will lower the harmonica one complete octave, so that it will sound something like a cello, or even a bass. The machine will be rotating at exactly half its normal speed of 33-1/3, but the harmonica will still be *in the same key* as it was originally. Obviously, this will make playing along, copying, or imitating a lot simpler. Incidentally, should you ever want to extract the *bass* part from a recording, this trick can be used in reverse. Just *speed* up the L.P. to 78 RPM. The song won't be in the same key, but the bass part will jump right out at you! Fantastic!

Playing In Any Key

As explained in the "Questions and Answers" *Harps* now come in *all* of the keys. If you can afford them all, fine! Unfortunately, many of us are not that rich. So, if you can come up with enough "bread" for *four Harps,* I would suggest that you get a **C, A, D,** and **G** *Harp. These harmonicas would pretty well cover you for most of the keys used and preferred by guitar players. It would also keep you in the second* position which would probably be most practical for *you.*

However, if you're going to be working with a piano player or an organist, it might be wise to get an **Eb** *Harp* as well. Keyboard players prefer to play Blues in **Bb,** which would be 2nd position on the **Eb** *Harp.*

The following table will specify the exact harmonica you'll need to play in *any* of the keys, in any one of *six* positions. Each position has all 12 keys listed. Decide in which position you want to play. Read *down* that column until you come to the key you need. Then read straight *across* to the last column on your *right.* The correct harmonica to use will be indicated in the appropriate box.

STRAIGHT HARP 1st Position	ALL THESE POSITIONS ARE CROSS HARP					HARMONICA REQUIRED
	2nd Position	3rd Position	4th Position	5th Position	6th Position	
A	E	B	C#(Db)	F#(Gb)	D	A
Bb	F	C	D	G	Eb	Bb
B	F#(Gb)	C#(Db)	Eb	G#(Ab)	E	B
C	G	D	E	A	F	C
Db(C#)	Ab(G#)	Eb	F	Bb	F#(Gb)	Db
D	A	E	F#(Gb)	B	G	D
Eb	Bb	F	G	C	Ab(G#)	Eb
E	B	F#(Gb)	G#(Ab)	C#(Db)	A	E
F	C	G	A	D	Bb	F
F#	C#(Db)	Ab(G#)	Bb	Eb	B	F#
G	D	A	B	E	C	G
Ab	Eb	Bb	C	F	C#(Db)	Ab

The keys with brackets around them sound exactly the same as the keys they're listed with. They're just "spelled" differently.

EXAMPLE: You want to play in the key of **E** in the 2nd position

1st Position	2nd Position	3rd Position	4th Position	5th Position	6th Position	HARMONICA REQUIRED
A	(E)	B	C#(Db)	F#(Gb)	D	A

You can also do this another way. Look *down* the HARMONICA REQUIRED column. Stop at the key of the harmonica on which you want to play. Then, looking across to the left, the chart will list all the possible keys in which that particular harp can play, and in the specific position.

The lowest sounding harmonica you can buy in the *Marine Band* category is the **G** *Harp*. From there they proceed up through the various keys in half steps until they reach the highest pitched *Harp* which is tuned in **F#**. Certain notes bend easier on the low harmonicas, while others seem to be more flexible on the higher harps. The possibilities are endless. Again the key word is *experiment!* You might try the newest harmonica of that breed, which is called the Golden Melody. On it I find the key of **A** *Harp* especially easy to handle, particularly where bending is involved. It's a fun harmonica.

If you've done your homework up to this point, you're probably ready for the "Special Effects" section where we'll tackle the various types of train effects, shakes, trills, vibrato, tremolo and other useful tricks.

Special Effects

THE TREMOLO

On the harmonica, the tremolo is probably the easiest and most useful effect of all. It should be noted though that the word itself has a somewhat different meaning when applied to certan *other* instruments. On the harmonica, it has come to mean a rapid fluctuation in the intensity or *volume* of a given note (or notes). *Tremolo,* on the mouth organ, should not be confused with *vibrato* in which the *pitch* is involved.

There are three ways that I know of to produce a *tremolo.* The easiest is to play the harmonica normally, while at the same time cupping and uncupping your right hand. (If you're a lefty, you can of course use your left.) The hand should pivot from the *wrists!* That's all there is to it! This can be done either by lipping or tongue blocking. It's especially useful and appropriate for folk, country, or just plain pretty music.

The second method, is what I call the "show-off" *tremolo.* Everything described in the first example applies, except that the arm pivots at the *elbow,* and the swings are very wide. It looks very impressive, certainly is showy, and it does sound a little different. Although this is not one of *my* favorites, it does appeal to some.

The third type of *tremolo* requires a bit more practice, and can only be produced in the lipping position. It sounds a little like a mandolin, because it results in the rapid repetition of a given note. This is accomplished by moving the tongue from side to side, while maintaining an even air stream. It is equally effective both BLOWING, and DRAWING. Used sparingly, with taste, it's a very useful device.

THE VIBRATO

This means the same thing for all instruments. The dictionary describes the *vibrato* as a "tremulous effect which is obtained by rapidly alternating the original tone with a slightly perceptible variation in *pitch*". This is what a violinist does when he pulsates his fingertip on a string. Another way to put it, is to think of a normal tone as a straight line looking like this: _____ A vibrato would then look like this: ‿‿‿‿‿‿‿

The *vibrato* can be produced either by lipping or tongue blocking. When performed in the lipping position, the sound resembles that of an oboe. Regardless of the method used, the sound originates in the throat. The silent syllable used is "yuh" repeated very rapidly like this "yuh-yuh-yuh-yuh-yuh-yuh-yuh". What you're actually doing is bending the tone very slightly in a pulsating fashion. Don't think of it as a "wah-wah", or it will slow down the pulse. This requires some practice. It is equally effective both in the BLOW and DRAW mode. Strangely, even though the upper register notes don't all bend, this effect, because of the pulsation, works perfectly fine both in the upper and the lower extremes of the harmonica.

TONGUING

NOTE: For all the following special tonguing effects, use the *LIPPING* method.

Single Tonguing

Used for sudden sharp attacks, and staccato cutoffs.
In the BLOW mode, articulate the sound "tut". If DRAWING say (silently, of course,) "hut". This effect works equally well with single notes and chords.

Double Tonguing

Used for repeated double note patterns that look like this musically: ♫ ♫ ♫ ♫ In the BLOW mode use the sound "tuk-ka" or "hut-ta". Whichever feels more natural to you. In the DRAW mode you can only use "hut-ta". (Personally, I prefer to articulate "hut-ta" for both BLOW and DRAW, since it's the same syllable combination and avoids confusion.)

Triple Tonguing

Excellent for playing 3 note groups either singly or repeated. ♪♪♪♪♪♪♪♪♪♪♪♪ This can be done with chords as well as with single notes. The syllables used in this case are "tuh-de-kuh", and the same sound is used both for BLOW and DRAW. (This combination of syllables may be a little difficult to articulate at first in the DRAW mode, but a bit of practice should cure that.) Triple tonguing can even be practiced silently without the harmonica. Try saying it in groups of three like this: "tuh-de-kuh   tuh-de-kuh   tuh-de-kuh   tut". The last one is a single tongue. (If you practice this without the harmonica, don't let anyone hear you, or they'll think you've flipped.)

THE SHAKE

This can be played either by tongue blocking, or lipping. On the harmonica, a *shake* has come to mean the rapid alternating of 2 notes *adjacent* to each other. These can either be both BLOW, or both DRAW. It's impossible to shake a BLOW DRAW combination. Musically, a shake might look like this:

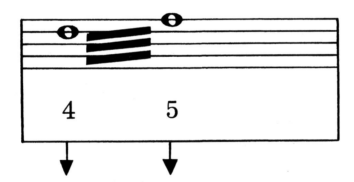

I've purposely picked the DRAW 4-5 combination because it's very often used when playing Blues in the 2nd position *Cross Harp*. (You can however use any combination you like.)

The easiest way to play a *shake* is to select either of the 2 notes you're going to use (it really doesn't matter whether you start on the higher or lower of the tones), then rapidly move the *Harp* back and forth to add the other note. Some players try to accomplish the same thing by moving their head! Forget it! Aside from getting dizzy you'd probably dislocate your vertebrae. Incidentally, you can bend both notes simultaneously while performing the *shake*. It's a wild, wailing sound and very useful. Learn how!

THE TRILL

For all practical purposes, *trills* are impossible on the *Marine Band* type of Harp. You can, however, *approximate* the *trill* on either of 2 BLOW notes. (BLOW 7 and 8) To create the effect, you have to bend the note you pick, BLOWING slightly harder than normal, and at the same time articulate the sound "yuh yuh yuh" very rapidly. The result sounds more like a yodel than a trill, and is of limited use at best....hardly worth the effort of learning to do it. If you think you can use it, fine!

THE TRAIN

A harmonica player who can't "make like a train", is like a ham sandwich without the ham! It's expected of you! And I know of three different ways to sound like a *train*.

In each of the following *train* effects, accent the *first* beat of each group. Start loud, and gradually increase speed. After sounding the whistle, continue at speed, but start to fade in volume, eventually becoming inaudible as the *train* disappears in the distance.

TYPE I TRAIN (STRAIGHT HARP)

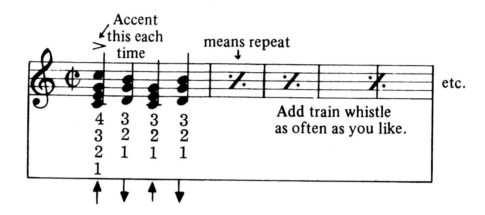

THE TRAIN WHISTLE. This effect is the same for *all* three train effects.

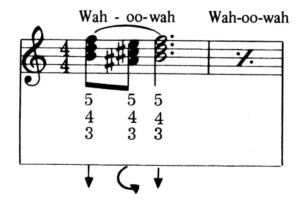

TYPE II TRAIN (CROSS HARP)

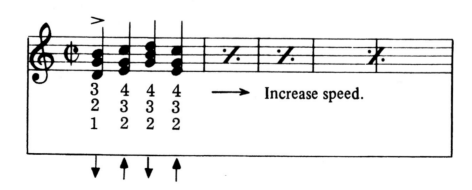

Exactly the same as Type I but in the cross harp position. This train starts on a DRAW CHORD.

You can also experiment by double tonguing each chord...it adds a bit more excitement.

TYPE III TRAIN

This is probably the best *train* effect of all, but is also the hardest to do. It uses only *one* chord in the BLOW mode. The chord is choked and cupped so that it almost loses all tonality. You only open the cupped hands for the accent on the first beat of each group. As you start to run out of air, sound the whistle, which will of course replenish your air supply. The speed of the effect is increased by articulating the sounds of "chukka chucka chucka" continuously until it becomes almost uncontrolled. This should continue until it becomes inaudible. Since all of this uses a lot of wind, you may have to resort to the whistle more often than in the other types of train effects.

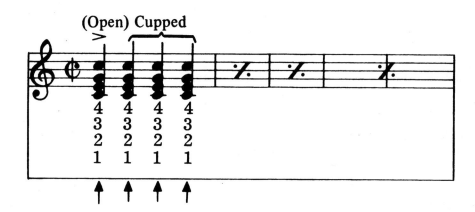

THE GROWL

Played in the lipping position only. For the *growl*, just play normally and at the same time roll your R the same as a classical singer would. (Your tongue actually vibrates if you do this right.) The effect works in the BLOW mode only. If you want to *growl* in the DRAW position, you literally have to *snore*. Very awkward, of limited value, and I wouldn't waste too much time on it.

THE TALKING HARMONICA

Years ago, a fellow by the name of Salty Holmes had a hit record in which his harmonica *talked*. Literally! It was on a 78 RPM disc and was released by London Records. It was called "I Found My Mama". In it, the harmonica formed words like "I wuv you." In addition, the harmonica also recited all of "Mary Had a Little Lamb". A girls voice would first establish the phrase, and then the harp would repeat it. The trick, of course, is to repeat the words *after* someone first *speaks* them, so that the recognition becomes definite.

To make your harp *talk*, the words must be articulated into the harmonica. Only certain reeds work with certain words, and only by experimentation can you determine the proper note to pick. Generally it's all kept in the lower register below hole 5, and always performed on DRAW notes. This effect will require much practice since it involves extremely controlled bending. Certainly worth working on. If nothing else, it will improve your bending technique tremendously.

THE GLISSANDO

This was explained at the beginning of the book.

Maintenance and Repair

Mechanically, the 10 hole diatonic harmonica is a relatively simple instrument, especially when we compare it to its larger more complicated relatives, like the reed organ or the accordian. Unlike them, the mouth organ has no keys, levers, springs, or other linkages that might be apt to malfunction. Accordingly, repairs are much easier to accomplish.

The harmonica consists of but five major components.

There are the two cover plates, front, and back.

— Front Cover Plate

— Back Cover Plate

Then we have two reed plates: BLOW, and DRAW.

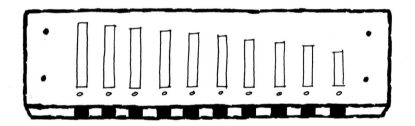

Blow *reed plate. Note that these reeds are* **inside** *the harmonica. (The rivets at the mouthpiece) low notes are at the left. The end of the reed that vibrates is, of course, the free end. (Opposite the rivet.)*

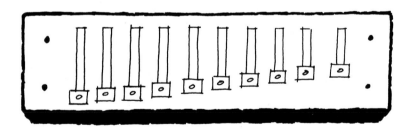

This is the **Draw** *reed plate. These reeds are clearly visible and accessible. The rivets, however, are now at the* **bottom** *of the harmonica. The vibrating end of the draw reed is at the mouthpiece. Making servicing much easier.*

Finally, there's one wooden comb on which this all fits.

The "Comb" generally made of wood. [Note nail holes.] Whenever re-assembling always fit nails into original holes for correct registration of reeds.

Basically, this is all you have to worry about, except of course for the nails, which hold all the parts together.

You will notice that the reed plates have ten reeds each. These are "fixed" reeds. That is, they are permanently riveted to the plate at the factory, and are not intended to be removed or changed. They can be tapped out and replaced by an expert, but this is certainly far beyond the scope of the average player, and is certainly *not* recommended. Besides, special tools are required, the procedure is time consuming, and results even for the "pro" are often unsatisfactory. Also when you send the harmonica to the factory for reed repairs, they replace *all* the reeds, so it seems silly to fool with replacement of a single reed.

Reeds are tuned by filing. To raise the pitch, the end of the reed is filed. To lower the pitch, the upper middle of the reed is filed.

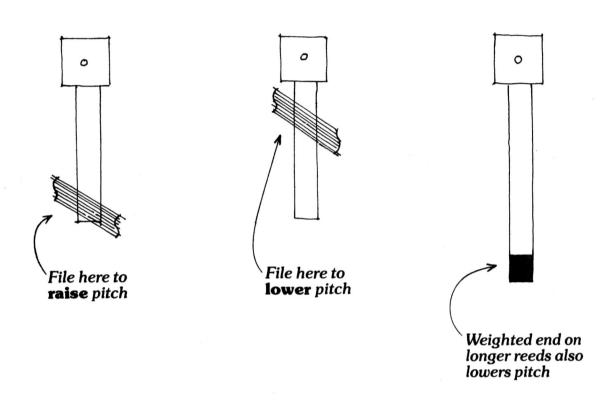

File here to **raise** *pitch*

File here to **lower** *pitch*

Weighted end on longer reeds also lowers pitch

In order for any reed to vibrate, it must be unobstructed, and free to move in its slot. It must also be slightly angled away from the reed plate so that the air stream will activate the reed. (More about this later.) Tolerances (or clearance if you prefer) between the reed and slot are very fine, so that even a speck of dust is enough to interfere with the vibration and result in jamming. That is why in this book, you will note that I continue to stress cleanliness, and also why it is so important to keep your harmonica in a case, or wrapped carefully when not in use.

If you were to remove the covers, you would see the reed plates. The reeds that are completely visible are the DRAW reeds. Those on the other side, in which slots only are seen, are the BLOW reeds. (Refer to the sketch at the beginning of this chapter which shows the differences quite clearly.)

Mechanically, both sets of reeds are quite identical, except for pitch and the fact that the BLOW reeds are riveted at the top and the DRAW reeds at the bottom.

Some of the longer reeds, you will notice, have an extra piece of metal on the ends. If you're wondering why, the answer is a simple one. It's there to add weight to the end of the reed, thereby slowing the rate of vibration. This in turn results in a lower note or pitch. If the weight were not added, the reed, in order to sound the same note, would have to be much larger. The harmonica then would have to be that much larger, and require a whole lot more wind. Obviously a very impractical harmonica would result. So, they add the weight!

All reeds are activated by an air stream. In the reed organ, it may be by an electrical pump, or by foot pedals. In the accordion, it's by the bellows. In the harmonica, it's accomplished by lung power, but in all cases, without the air, we couldn't generate a continuous tone.

One more thing you should know, and then you'll be able to go on to actual repairs. I refer to the function of the wooden comb. Not only do the partitions separate the actual notes, but they also serve an additional purpose. They form the sound chambers in which the various reeds resonate. Each chamber services two reeds, a BLOW, and a DRAW. If you did not have these sound chambers, and were to BLOW a reed just on the reed plate, the sound would be very thin, weak, and ineffectual.

Now that you know all about *how* the harmonica works, we can go on to practical maintenance and repair.

A good basic rule to follow when making repairs is: NEVER TAKE THE HARMONICA APART UNLESS ABSOLUTELY NECESSARY! Most repairs can be completed without removing even the cover plates. Another thing to remember: Once you take the harmonica apart, you void the guarantee, so if you think you've purchased a defective instrument, and it's still new, by all means send it back to the factory. If it's their fault, they'll fix it.

Symptom: The wooden partitions have swelled so that they protrude above the cover plates, and interfere with playing.

Solution: Lay the harmonica on its side on a flat surface, and with a very sharp razor blade, trim the parts that are protruding, being sure to cut downward. A single edged blade is probably a lot safer than a double, and also easier to use. Be sure not to let any wood fragments fall into the harmonica. Also, don't cut lengthwise along the harmonica, or you may snap the partitions.

Trim in this direction only

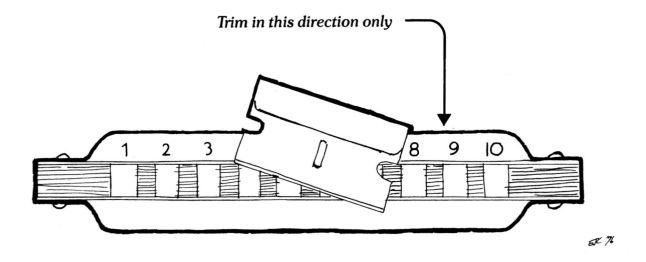

Symptom: A note is stuck and no amount of tapping will clear it. It simply will not respond.

Solution: The first thing to try is rapid *hard* BLOWING and DRAWING. Your mouth should cover several holes while doing this, including, of course, the faulty note. Very often this will work. If it does not, then we go further. What we do is improvise a simple tool out of an ordinary (medium sized) safety pin. First straighten it out, and then with a pair of pliers, bend the point about 1/8th of an inch from the end, at right angles to the pin. It should look like this:

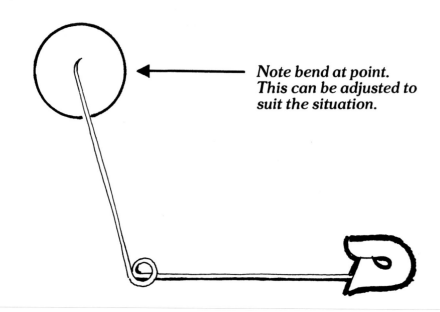

Note bend at point. This can be adjusted to suit the situation.

If the stuck reed is a BLOW reed, insert the pin *very carefully* from the *bottom* of the harmonica, between the covers and the reed plate. (Don't remove the covers for this.) Now very gently, using the point of the tool, prod the reed that's jammed, pushing toward the *inside* of the harmonica. If the covers have been bent, or if for any other reason your *Harp* does not have enough clearance to insert the pin, you'll have to remove the covers. (Read further for that procedure.) But whether the cover plates remain on or are taken off, the technique is the same. Be sure to keep in mind that the BLOW reeds are those whose rivets are visible from the *top* of the fully assembled harmonica. Also remember that pressure on a reed is always applied to the end of the reed furthest from the rivet.

If the problem reed should happen to be a DRAW reed, the fix is easier. You can definitely reach a DRAW reed without removing the covers. Again, remember that the DRAW reeds are those whose rivets are visible from the *bottom* of the harmonica. In this situation, simply insert the bent pin into the *tone chamber* of the affected note. Push the end of the reed very gently toward the *outside* of your *Harp*. Incidentally, you don't have to probe very deeply for this, since the flexing end of the DRAW reed is at the top (the opposite end from the rivet). In both the DRAW and BLOW notes, the reed should not be pushed more than a fraction of an inch. As a matter of fact, the higher the note, the smaller the reed, and the smaller the reed, the less flexible it is, which simply means it cannot be moved as far as a larger reed. So guide yourself accordingly. (Basically what you're trying to accomplish is to dislodge any dirt, dust, foreign matter, or dried saliva that might be interfering with the normal action of the reed.) If, after all these efforts, the *Harp* still won't work, it can only be due to a badly swollen comb, or a misaligned reed. In either case, you're in over your head. Send the harmonica back to the factory, and let the professionals fix it for you.

Generally speaking, these are the problems that will arise most often. Once you learn to handle these, if you want to go further, you can tackle the more involved repairs, such as adjusting response, removing rattles, touching up burrs, and even tuning reeds that have dropped in pitch. However, you will need some special tools, as well as special "know-how" to accomplish this. The basic tools are generally available in any well equipped hardware store. First you'll need a set of jewelers files, of the assorted variety (round, flat, knifelike, etc.). Then, in order to see what you're doing, you'll require a jewelers "loop" or any other type of magnifying lens which leaves both hands free. Equally necessary is a small screwdriver with a shank thin enough to fit into the holes of the harmonica. (This is used as a backup to keep the reeds from bending when they're being tuned from the outside.) And finally, you'll use a couple of razor blades and a simple penknife. You may eventually improvise your own tools, but in many years at this sort of thing, I've found that I can complete almost any repair with the tools mentioned.

In all of the procedures that follow, the covers (or cover plates) must be removed. While this is quite simple to do, the utmost care should be taken not to bend or deform the covers in any way. Using the large blade of your penknife, carefully slip the blade under the nails (between the reed plates and the covers), and slowly pry the covers off. Needless to say, don't cut yourself. Be sure that you put the nails in a safe place so that you'll have them for re-assembly. Incidentally, when you put the covers back on again, *don't* use a hammer to drive the nails home. What I find most effective is a pair of slip joint pliers, and I position the nails, one side at a time, and simply press them into place, using the pliers as a sort of vise. This eliminates the possibility of mashing the plate with an ill-directed hammer blow, and also the chance of knocking a reed out of alignment.

Once the covers have been removed, identify the affected reed. If you don't do this, chances are that you'll find yourself operating on a perfectly good reed. What I generally do is make a tiny scratch with the point of a file on the reed plate. This effectively isolates the note in question, and I can proceed without wondering whether or not I have the sick reed.

Symptom: The reed rattles, or buzzes.

Solution: BLOW or DRAW on the affected reed with the covers off. Has the buzz disappeared? If the answer is yes, then it must be caused by bent or warped covers. This is usually the result of grasping the harp too hard. Gradually the cover plates deform, and eventually interfere with the reed. Nothing much you can do then except try to bend the covers back into line. Usually this does not work, because the top bends as well, causing leaks. So the cure becomes worse than the illness. New cover plates are called for - a factory job.

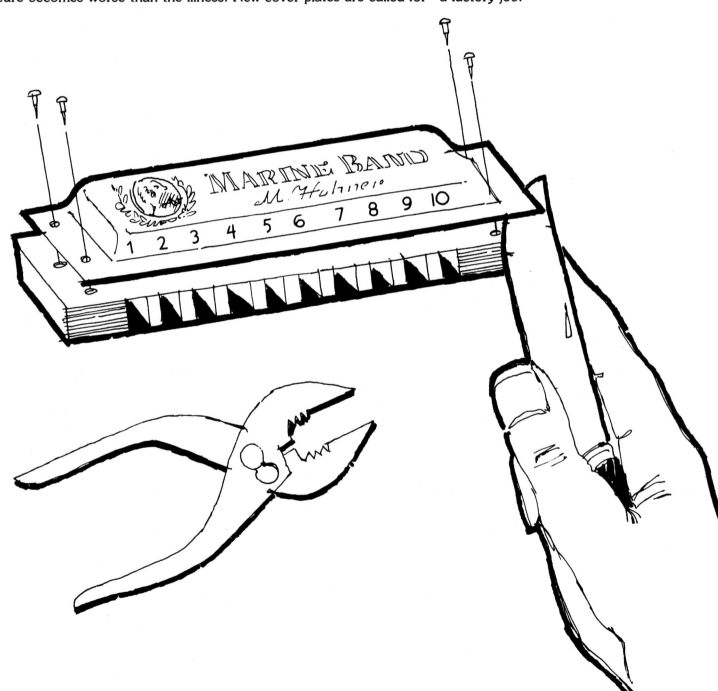

If the buzz or rattle is still apparent, then it is usually the result of a slight burr on the reed, or sometimes the reed is barely contacting a swollen comb during its vibration. This is where you use your magnifier. If the reed in question is a DRAW, you can observe it directly. Gently push the reed so that it's parallel to the reed plate. Is there equal space all around? Is any part of the reed touching? As you move it to and fro does it contact the slot? If the answer is yes, then the burr will have to be trimmed off. For this a file is used. (I generally prefer a knife file.) With a razor blade under the reed (see sketch), very gently remove the burr. If the note is a BLOW, the procedure is exactly the same except that the reed plate *has to be removed!* I generally advise against that, since as explained earlier in this book, it's a very tricky procedure, even for the pro. However, if you want to try, this is the way it's done: first, using the wide blade of your pocket knife, gently pry the reed plate off, being exceedingly careful not to groove the wooden comb as you pry, or you'll cause air leaks. Once the plate is off, you'll notice that the *inside* of the BLOW reed plate looks exactly like the outside of the DRAW plate, except for the positioning of the rivets. All repair details then become identical. Check for burrs with your magnifier, and proceed as you did for the DRAW notes.

Whenever filing a reed it is preferrable to use a double-edged razor blade so that the file can work unobstructed.

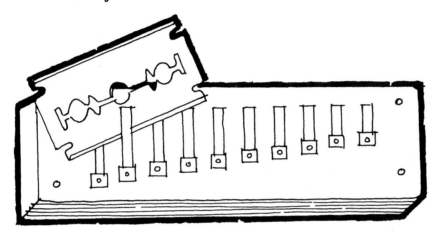

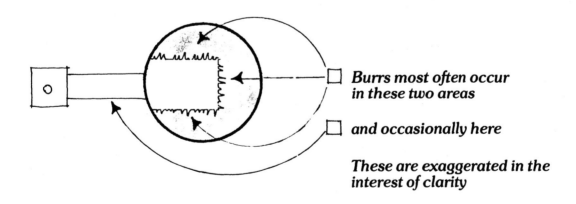

Burrs most often occur in these two areas

and occasionally here

These are exaggerated in the interest of clarity

If, during your inspection, you noticed that the reed was contacting the wooden comb, I suggest you send the harmonica to the factory. This particular fix requires shaving of the comb, removal of the reed plates of course, realignment of those plates. Besides, if the comb is too badly swollen, the factory will generally replace it; all in all, a much better deal for you.

Incidentally, if you remove the reed plates for any reason, be sure to try to reposition them on the comb *exactly* as they were originally. If you don't, you may very well jam the reeds, as well as cause all sorts of compression leaks. When putting the plates back on, put the nails in the original holes and gently press them home with a pair of slip joint pliers.

Symptom: The note is out of tune (gone flat).

Solution and Explanation: There are two ways that a note goes out of tune. The first is when suddenly, while you're playing, the reed drops several tones, and as you check it, it continues to slide down. That reed has *had it!* Nothing you can do! It's dead! Kaput! Finished! It has succumbed to metal fatigue, which is always fatal. You either junk the harp, use it for spare parts, or send it in for repairs.

The other way that a reed goes flat is more subtle. Generally it will go unnoticed for quite a time, because it happens very gradually. Sometimes it will be a note that is bent more often than the others, or it may be a note that is stressed a little bit harder. This problem will almost always respond to therapy, and quite logically the treatment consists of tuning the reed back to health.

If the reed is a DRAW reed, the fix is comparatively simple. First, of course, isolate the reed by scratching a mark on the plate, so that you know *exactly* which reed you want to work on. Then slide a double edged razor blade under the reed. Be very careful not to force the razor too far toward the rivet since you don't want to deform the reed in any way.

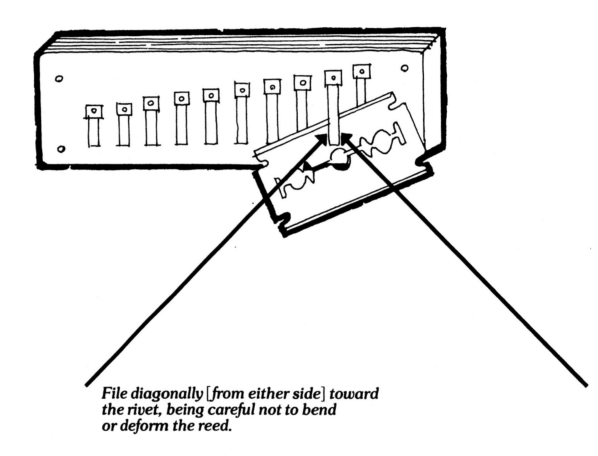

File diagonally [from either side] toward the rivet, being careful not to bend or deform the reed.

Using great care, file the *end* of the reed, filing at a slight angle *toward* the rivet, which helps to minimize burrs. (If in any doubt, refer to sketch above.) Don't make more than one or two light passes with the file, and then check the note for correct pitch. If you remove too much material, you'll wind up with a reed that's *sharp*, which is just as bad as one that's flat, so proceed slowly! If you should accidentally overdo, all is not lost. Refer again to sketch on p. 39, which illustrates the method of lowering pitch; then carefully remove just enough material from the upper *center* portion of the reed to bring it into correct tune. In all operations where filing is necessary, try to avoid leaving burrs on the reed. Always check this with your magnifier, and if none are apparent and you have no buzzing sounds, you're in good shape.

Symptom: The note does not respond at all under sudden attack, or when blown hard. It does, however, work just fine when played softly.

Solution: This is a classic symptom which occurs quite often, and can be remedied quite easily. It is caused by insufficient offset of the reed.

Look Along Edge of Reed Plate   (All diagrams exaggerated for clarity.)

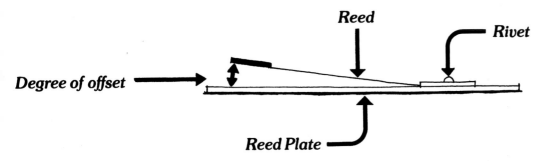

Degree of offset   *Reed*   *Rivet*   *Reed Plate*

Almost no offset

This reed probably wouldn't respond at all, or if it did, only if played very, very softly.

Too much offset

*This reed **would** respond, but only if played very hard. It would **not** respond to soft playing.*

The happy compromise. Offset is correctly set

*This reed will respond to **both** soft and hard playing. If you prefer to play **very** hard, you can add even more offset.*

Incidentally, if a reed has *no* offset, it won't respond at all! Too little offset, and the note will only sound when played very softly. By the same token, if the reed has too much, it will only play when attacked very hard, and won't sound at all when blown softly. (This of course applies to DRAW notes as well.)

The ideal solution is to find the happy medium where the reed will respond to both loud and soft playing equally well. How do you find this correct setting? Actually, it isn't as difficult as it may sound. Start by comparing the offending reed with any adjoining reed of roughly the same size. There will be an obvious difference in the offset. It then remains for you to adjust the note that's giving the trouble so that it resembles the adjoining note that works. Since we're talking about tiny fractions of an inch, your magnifier will come in handy for this. If the note is a DRAW, simply lift, or flex the end of the reed slightly, but be very careful not to BEND it! This may sound like a contradiction, but it really isn't, because if the note is lifted too far, it will visibly bend out of shape, and that's fatal! All you need is just enough to correct the offset. When you lift, just flex the reed far enough so that you can still feel the springiness and resistance of the reed; then check again. At first, this will be purely a trial and error operation, but after a few tries, it becomes quite simple. This particular fix will prove very useful.

Should the troublesome reed happen to be a BLOW reed, everything works exactly the same, but in reverse. That is, the offset is increased by *pushing the reed in* toward the comb. In any event removal of the reed plate is *not* necessary! Offset inspection for BLOW notes is equally simple. Just squint down the reed slot with your magnifier, looking toward the end of the reed. Offset spacing then becomes easily visible.

Again, I must stress care, caution, and attention to details. They'll pay off in satisfactory results.

Perhaps one day, you'll discover shortcuts and new methods that may simplify these procedures even more. Until then, we trust this chapter on repairs will prove helpful in clearing up some of the myths and in solving some of the problems that so often plague harmonica players.

Electronics, Amplification Microphones and Accessorie.

The science of electronics has come so far in recent years that to cover it adequately would take several books, let alone one chapter. However, as it relates to the harmonica, we can eliminate the unnecessary technical details, and just stick to those areas that are useful to us.

AMPLIFICATION

No instrument I know of can benefit more from amplification than the harmonica. With the proper amplifier, a harmonica can be heard above a symphony orchestra.

Amplifiers come in all shapes and sizes, and at prices ranging from about $30.00 to as much as you want to pay. (Some of the popular Rock groups have been know to carry as much as $150,000.00 worth of amplification and sound equipment!)

The more expensive amplifiers are generally made up of solid state components (no tubes) and have all sorts of built in "goodies" like reverberation (echo effects) and tremolo electronically produced. Some even have a built in "fuzz" unit, which is a type of distortion sometimes used by guitar players to create a raucous, raunchy sound.

The better amplifiers are also available with two or more channels. Each channel has individual controls, so that one or more instruments can plug into the same amplifier, yet still maintain individual control of each instrument.

The type of amplifier you should buy depends on how you want to use it. If you want to fill a large auditorium with sound, you'll require a fairly powerful unit, but *don't* buy more power than you need. Even the smallest of amplifiers puts out an amazing amount of sound.

The built-in feature that is most effective with the *Harp* is the reverberation or echo unit. It tends to smooth out the sound of the harmonica, making it much rounder and more mellow. It really enhances the overall effect tremendously.

Also available are add-on echo units that again come in all types and sizes. The best of these generally use a continuous loop of tape, and the resulting echo can be delayed or repeated to create all sorts of unusual sounds and effects obtainable in no other way.

The built-in electronic tremolo is of limited use at best, where the *Harp* is concerned. I've never found much use for it. Incidentally, amplifiers, add-ons and microphones can all be tried out in the store before purchase, so you can always pick the units you like best. Since you have many to choose from, you should be able to come up with a winner!

MICROPHONES

There are literally hundreds of microphones to pick from. There are crystal mikes, throat mikes, dynamic, condenser, cardioid, ribbon, even FM wireless microphones, and probably some types I haven't run across yet! The list does seem confusing, but it need not be.

The first rule: Don't buy more microphone than you need. The most expensive is not necessarily the best sounding where your mouth organ is concerned. For instance, some of the more costly mikes can reproduce sounds as low as 20 cycles per second (Hz) and as high as 16,000 Hz. Most of us can't even hear past 13,000. The top note on the highest sounding harmonica is an **F#**. It vibrates at only 3153.96 Hz! (How's that for being precise?) And the lowest note on the key of **G** *Marine Band* oscillates at 196 Hz. So why pay for all that unnecessary range that you can't possibly use? Even the cheapest mikes will cover the harmonica register adequately. It then becomes a matter of picking the one that sounds best to you. Be sure to test several different types, preferably with the amplifier you'll be using. Play with the Bass and Treble controls (on the amplifier). Guided by cost and intended use, you'll find it fairly easy to make a choice.

CRYSTAL MIKES

The simple crystal mikes are very cheap and usually come with some sort of fitting or clamp for attaching to the harmonica. These work surprisingly well for their minimal cost, but *all* contact microphones pick up extraneous sounds like lip smacking and hand sliding. Hohner sells one that's adjustable (Model HH9911) and Lafayette Radio advertizes a crystal mike just made for the harmonica at a ridiculously low price. This type of microphone does tend to emphasize the "highs". Personally, I have used a simple crystal cartridge (available from most mail order electronic outlets) and *taped* it to the *bottom* of the harp with masking tape. It worked just fine! Contact devices do limit your cupping, tremolo and other techniques, since once they're attached, that's it!

THROAT MIKES

Not many stores carry throat mikes, although some groups use them. The good ones are expensive. They fit against the throat and have a somewhat unique sound.

DYNAMIC, CARDIOID, RIBBON, AND CONDENSER MIKES

Although technically each of these mikes works on a slightly different principle, for our purposes they fall into the same category, since they are either held in the hand while playing, or attached to a mike stand. All work very well, but have individual characteristics. Generally, ribbon and cardioids tend to make the *Harp* sound rounder, and fatter, while condenser mikes appear to stress the highs. To repeat, it's all a matter of taste.

DIRECTIONAL AND OMNI-DIRECTIONAL MIKES

An omni-direction mike will pick up sound from many directions, while the directional has a very narrow pick-up pattern. For the harmonica playing solo, a directional would be the better choice, since it would screen out or minimize unwanted sound. On the other hand, if you have several players using one microphone, you'd naturally benefit from the characteristics of the omni-directional mike.

TECHNIQUE

Many *Blues Harp* players prefer to play with the microphone cupped in the hand, so that the mike can be manipulated as desired. Other professionals use the mike on a stand, since they feel they have more control *that* way. When it's on a stand, the microphone doesn't get in the way when you want to use a hand tremolo, or if you want to back off and then close in for contrast. It also allows you to have better control of the cupping technique. Again, "different strokes for different folks". As long as you know what the options are, you can pick what's best for you.

The electronic "octave splitter" devices which are so popular with flute and woodwind players, do *not* work with the harmonica. If you really want to get into far out sounds, you should experiment with the electronic synthesizers. But that's a whole different bag.

If you're talented enough to be able to play the guitar, and want to play both guitar and harmonica at the same time, there are a couple of models of The Elton Harmonica Holder available. Model #HHA 450 clamps on the side of the guitar, works very well, and is adjustable to any angle. Model #HHA 150 is also adjustable, but it fits the shape of the neck. Both of these are available from M. Hohner. (Obviously, if you want to use either of these with a microphone, you would have to use a mike stand.)

The Chromatic Harmonicas

Although this book is primarily intended to focus on the diatonic types of harmonicas, a brief description of the *Chromatics* may prove both enlightening and helpful. It should also clear up any misconceptions you may have about what they can and can't do.

Chromatic harmonicas differ from the diatonic (*Marine Band*) type in that they provide complete twelve-note octaves. These contain all the sharps and flats. (The diatonic harmonicas have a seven note octave.) In order to provide this twelve note octave, each hole contains *four* reeds: a BLOW reed and a DRAW reed for the two *natural* notes, and a BLOW reed and a DRAW reed for the two chromatic notes. This makes it possible to play in *any* key on one instrument. Diatonics, on the other hand, only have *two* reeds in each hole, and *no* built-in sharps or flats.

HOW THEY WORK

Mechanically speaking, a chromatic harmonica is really two diatonic harmonicas tuned one half-step apart, and placed one above the other. On a C harmonica, this would include the key of **C** and **C#**. Chromatic tones are obtained by pressing a spring loaded button on the end of the instrument. With the button in the out or natural position, the diatonic scale(s) of the key of **C** becomes available. When the button is pressed in, you get the scale of **C#**. This combination of both diatonic scales makes possible every tone in the chromatic compass. These harmonicas all contain plastic valves which keep you from using too much breath. They stop the air from leaking through the reed channels. This also results in increased volume.

THE DIFFERENT TYPES

THE KOCH HARMONICA (Chromatic)

All chromatic harmonicas except the Koch are solo tuned, which means each group of four holes covers a complete octave. The Koch, however, is tuned exactly like the *Marine Band*. Unlike the Marine Band, which has only twenty reeds, the Koch has forty. It also has ten holes, is fully chromatic, and is available in the keys of **C** or **G**. (If you were to play your **C** Koch with the button always pressed in, you would have the perfectly fine equivalent of a **C#** *Marine Band*. If you did the same thing with a **G** Koch, you'd have a diatonic harmonica in the key of **Ab (G#)**. The catalog number for this instrument is HH980.)

THE CHROMONICA HH260

This type is similar to the Koch, but is *solo* tuned and encompasses two and a half octaves. It also has ten holes and forty reeds.

THE SUPER CHROMONICA HH270

This is probably the most popular chromatic harmonica and is the choice of most, but not all, professionals. This instruments boasts *three* complete octaves, plus an additional high **C#** and **D**. Its range, which starts with middle **C** is actually greater than that of a flute! This model is available in the key of **A, Bb, C, D, E, F,** and **G**. I believe additional keys can be specially ordered. (Most of the Pros I know, myself included, prefer this model in the key of **C** for reading music and for normal playing. Some of the other keys are lower and more mellow sounding, which might be more desirable for special uses.)

THE 64 CHROMONICA HH280

This is the Big Daddy of them all! The range of this unique instrument starts from an octave below middle **C** and continues for an incredible four octaves. It even includes two additional notes (**C#** and **D**). I know of no other wind instrument of any size that even approaches this range. (The accordion doesn't count; its a bellows instrument.)

There is another new chromatic harmonica in the final stages of development that you should know about. This instrument will reflect the first really radical change in harmonica design in many years. The first models will have a four octave range. It is to be called *The Professional 2016 CBH*. (The initials are for its designer, Chamber Huang.) This chromatic will be completely different in appearance, as well as in construction.

I had the pleasure of playing one of the first prototypes, and found it to have much better compression and resonance than its predecessors. This interesting instrument should be available by the time you read this.

There are many other chromatic harmonicas, some of which don't have a button and are used for special effects, or for Band work. There are also Bass harmonicas, chord harmonicas, specially tuned *Harps*, and so forth. Unfortunately, space does not allow us to explore every model, so we've tried to choose those that we think might have the most interest for you. There is, however, a comprehensive catalog available, for a minimal charge, from M. Hohner, Andrews Road, Hicksville, N.Y. 11802. It lists all of their models, including many types not described in this book. Ask for catalog 1024.

By the way, don't let anyone tell you that you can't play Blues on a chromatic harmonica! Nothing could be further from the truth. While it is true that you cannot duplicate the sound of the DRAW chord on the *Marine Band* (except for the Koch chromatic), the additional sharps, flats, trills, and chord effects that are possible more than make up for this. Almost *anything* can be played on the chromatic. It just takes more practice and know-how.